REPORTING FROM
NIGHT

REPORTING FROM
NIGHT

KATERI LANTHIER

Copyright© Kateri Lanthier, 2011

Published by Iguana Books
460 Richmond St. West, Ste 401
Toronto, Ontario
M5V 1Y1

All rights reserved. No part of this publication may be reproduced or transmitted in any form or by any means, electronic, mechanical, recording or otherwise (except brief passages for purposes of review) without the prior permission of the author.

Permission to photocopy should be requested from Access Copyright.

This is the Original Print Edition of Reporting from Night.

Library and Archives Canada Cataloguing in Publication

Lanthier, Kateri
Reporting from night / Kateri Lanthier.

Poems.
Also issued in electronic format.
ISBN 978-0-9866838-8-6

I. Title.

PS8623.A69878R47 2011   C811'.6   C2011-908044-3

Cover design by Rolf Busch
Cover art by Douglas Walker: *Untitled #A-195*, oil on panel, 44 x 32 in.
Courtesy of Douglas Walker. www.douglaswalker.ca
Interior design by Lea Kaplan

2 4 6 8 9 7 5 3 1

For Nicholas, Julia and William

In memory of my mother, Jane

Table of Contents

Part I: Earth's Familiar Objects

Poor Butterfly	2
Beached	3
Wasn't Listening	4
Royal Icing	5
Politicos	6
Romance	7
Covet	8
Museum of Days	9
Owlish	10
Winter Inventions, Alberta	11
Telling	12
Beauty's Danger	13
Exit/Entrance	14
New, Again	15
El Anatsui: Wall Sculptures	16
Decorated	17
Ravine	18
Road Trip	19
Gulled	20
Shuttled	21
Books Were	22
Spiked	23
Oscar Wilde at the City Auditorium	24
Circus 1907	25

Part II: Who is Us

Cygnet Lake	28
Table Fable	30
Small Hours	31
Lullaby of Off-Off-Broadway	32
Winter Garden: Performances Daily	33
Year of the Rabbit	34
Reporting from Night	35
Milk Tooth	36
Imprinted	38
Late	39
Copper Cliff	41
Lost Taut Line	42
Nov. 5:15 pm	43
Snail's Pace	44
Morning Kindergarten.	45
Night Cartographer's Song	46
Demi-monde	47
March Hatter	48
Numb	49
Drawing In	50
Night Undone	51
Martial	52
Lake Road Knowledge	53
The Near Suburbs	54
Wiskatjan	56
English Drama to 1642	57
Cooler Heads	58
In Arcadia	59
Bedtime Story	61
Envoi	62
Acknowledgements	63

Wild Nights – Wild Nights!
Were I with thee
Wild Nights should be
Our luxury!

- Emily Dickinson

1
Earth's Familiar Objects

All memory we owe to objects
- Piotr Sommer

Q. What is the job of a flower?

From Reading Activity #5,
Grade 3 biology worksheet

A. Sonnets, brides, *parfumeries*, tattoos. Memorials, honey. Still, life.

Poor Butterfly

Stifled heartbeat wings.
Drunk on blood,
sweat and tears, or so
they've all been told
one time too many
down at the conservatory/
lab/
zinc bar.

Huge butterflies meander
like indecisive birds.

Can't help if I prefer
the hummingbird's
lost lyrics
or the avidity of the chickadee.

Beached

1. Sun, stroke

What we prized on Lake Ontario shores:
dinosaur jaw, shark teeth, quartz orbs
and goblin ore. Cobalt slivers
of Blue Willow, the crockery smashed
by scullery maids
and washed, washed,
washed to the bone.

Rocks balanced *en pointe*
by beach-stone technicians.
Couples in jean shorts danced to recorded salsa.
Our stroller did the boardwalk wobble.
Dazed on the sand,
daylight stargazers felt the slow burn.
Rochester obliged as the near horizon.

Waves sent a foaming bottle-message.
Clouds chest-pumped mountain impressions.
The beach walked home in our sandals.

2. After party

Fog appropriate for Day One.
Can we really see you yet, New Year?
Lake Ontario a few yards wide,
the rest is *all spaced out.*
Champagne cork bobs ashore.
Ice, on the rocks,
takes a boot to the head.
Condom sleeps on sand,
a spent shrivel.
Ducks are bottoms up.

Wasn't Listening

All that we never held dear
has cost us far too much.

The aftermath
rarely adds up.

The last train is parked in the shunt yard.
The airport, you've heard, is deserted.
The river is rising.

Air seems to have left the room.

Where is the delicate rain?

Royal Icing

Crowned heads roll along the tarmac.
Lilacs-in-waiting curtsy by the chain link.
We offer cake of elephantine splendour
and redcoats on the hoof.

Pretender to the Monarch,
this Painted Lady.
Social butterflies
snapped by the paps.

Uncommon wealth,
not of our world.
Amuse us.

Politicos

Scare quotes, scarecrows, sacred cows
ripped from the headlines,
tossed in the bin. A real mess,
this time, unrecyclable.
Kids are making mountains out of mudhills.
It's all one big smear campaign here.

A Sargasso sea of
celebutantes, starchitects,
those who fall upward.
Champers on the balcony
chanters below.
GPS led us
wrong way down the runway.
The police put on the kettle
in the rain.
It beggars belief
in the bomb-proof bunker.
The liar in his lair,
a hideous hideout
of Corinthian concrete.

Even if we're not invited to the party,
we should go as
unsuspecting
guests.

Romance

Our evensong, nightlight, aubade:
the drone, roar, flicker, flash, drone
of the snowplow.
Dark slick streets kiss
the coruscating snow.

Covet

A diamond cache
on the wrong side of the window.
Garnet pomegranate
seeds slip through our fingers
Icicles turn topaz
from 5:45 to 5:50 pm or 7:45 to 7:50 am, *only*.
Amethyst turret of a crayon,
mad castle in a box, all peaks, no rooms.
Your ruby cheeks startle strangers on the street.
Back indoors, they dim
to opal.

Museum of Days

Hammered-silver waves, rough repoussé.
Gold-leafed hopscotch rocket
leap-frogging the Tollund-Man-banana
peel, bog-soaked black.
Ancient lunch, ossified crusts.

The kindergarten girls dressed for butterfly theatre.
Their mothers like mourning weeds.

On the early maple, leaves like late-summer
peaches. October light
in September.

Sidewalk, sedimentary,
leached by tears,
all pockmark and glitter.

Owlish

Our grey cat is an animist of dust
Herding hoarded ghost mice.

Our grey cat is an activist of dust
Camping in a nest of herself.

Our grey cat is an archivist of dust
Swivel-necked, looking to the future.

Winter Inventions, Alberta

In the winter hot-spring
I wear icicle dreadlocks.
My breasts are steam.
Your fiery toes find my ankle
at the earth's boiling core.

From a canvas sack
hidden below stairs
a storekeeper scatters salt.
Burning pearls
rattle at our feet.

With a hockey helmet hooked over
the stick at his shoulder
a seven-year-old is a thirties hobo,
a soldier slinging a captured skull.

When a girl shovels snow
her jacket flares
with the fuchsia blooms
of southern beaches.
Her dog leaps for the ice
in the wild spray.

As I leave town,
my pickup truck slides
on black ice, startling
the elk, their rumps curled up
in a sneer, white against brown
of a whittled twig,
a broken almond.

House lights across the field
are an astral blue-green
like the dashboard lights.
When I lean forward
distant houses reveal
the speed at which I travel,
what little fuel remains.

Telling

Aesop asleep in the shadows.
Grimm light in the clearing.
Arthur Rackham trees
crowd the ravine.
Needle-nosed,
stoop-shouldered, quizzical of eye,
tattered leaf dresses and all.

You dreamed of "an owl
that was golden all over. We were having tea.
Then you brought us biscuits.
The wrong kind."

A knight in shining armor lolls
in the back of the dumptruck,
anteater noses elephant,
two fire-breathing dragons guard the giant
ladybug, uncoupled
train cars bury
the plastic pony palace.

On a windowsill, a rhino, a platypus, and a jellyfish
try to make sense
of the leafless oaks and maples—and each other.
Later, much later,
they'll all walk into a bar.

All the way home,
you stepped in and out
of my shadow.

Beauty's Danger

A collage of a mermaid wearing a shell
"full of perfume that makes you
so sleepy."
A sculpture of notched, painted Popsicle sticks.
"Blues going to one green. It's a tree
hunters were shooting at."

We have a Parisian pumpkin,
"with a scar, like Madeline
after she had her appendix out."

As we strolled past the mannequins,
you said, "This is the fashion store
for ladies with no heads."

Exit/Entrance

A boy tripped on the stairs
on the last day of school, dropping clay
-made bones, a surgeon's tray full.
Miniature skeleton
clattered down,
tricking random kids
into three-legged races.
Loose limbs danced to
the heavy
glass doors,
limning
summer,
limbing
escape.

Squashed sandwiches, sweat,
paint, chalk and gravel:
the hallway promises
to hold the bouquet.
Sneaker-squeak reverb.
One limp, lost boot.

Two months later,
once again,
every third kid
leaps
from the third-last
step.

New, Again

Cradling moon,
new again,
soon outgrown.

Wan light.
Swanlight.
Ugly-duckling April.

Sprincognito.
The shiver
in a tulip's tunic.

This pity party
ends in rain
or May.

El Anatsui: Wall Sculptures

Kente cloth stitched from chain mail,
a golden hive,
liquor bottle caps like a million
wincing faces,
magnificent robes, scarred flags,
continents that ripple and shift.

Decorated

Matryoshka, one virginal birth
within another, pose on the mantel,
indifferent to straight-backed
slack-jawed Nutcracker militia.
The tree's all baubled out.
But these are sugared-glass shards
to the sunset's glow
between two oaks,
or the light it cast
on our faces.

Ravine

1.

By day, we watch it.
In the evening, we listen to it.
At night, we step outside
to feel its breath.

2.

All the discarded party dresses.
Who knew the trees were having so much fun?

The more leaves are lost,
the more lights we see at night.
In the cold,
the city glimmers through the trees.

Road Trip

Heavily oaked,
this heavenly 'hood.
Late-summer foliage
charms cheap Chardonnay.

Sweet-talking sourpuss.

Shadowy lace shattered
by a toy car veering
off-ramp, landing face-
bumper-first
in the glass.
Gulp. Smash.

Gulled

by a spring-like thaw.
Mocking freewheelers
cased the schoolyard,
vocal track underscored
by high-pitched kids. Then snow
feathers scattered.
Burst pillow,
dream over.

Shuttled

Everyone's backs turned
to the beach.

Go/no go/gone.

Gorgeous useless wonder.

Negative return.
The apogee.

The camera's steady gaze at Earth.

Books Were

songs,
then masonry,
coracles,
treen,
candles.
foliage,
saddles,
blankets,
shirtwaists,
slurry.
Now served under glass.

Spiked

Coarse-pored, well-travelled,
overly cheerful lemons.
You gathered them before I arrived.

And buckwheat honey like a slurred compliment.
Glass pitcher, bathed and wearing loose beads.

The tribal rug that chafed bare legs.
The Berlioz for my adolescent taste.

Your shutters were open for an audience
in the branches. Trees in the heat.

Toppled tomes.
I tried to read spines

while the letters slid.
My sundress, too:
unchaperoned.

Your eyes, shimmering.
Your "unknown thirst."

Ice needling
my tongue.

The tart reply
I swallowed.

Oscar Wilde at the City Auditorium
(Belleville, Ontario, 1882)

The next night, she swung an orange lamp
of lilies in flared-lip circles through the garden.
Her tortoiseshell comb
barely held on by the teeth.
Gossiping near the bonfire, green leaves,
scorched, censored themselves.

She won't go in.
She will wear a porcupine quill
behind one ear, or prick a finger to let fall
a red drop on the red floor of pine.
Her secrets are scrolled in birchbark,
posted in the rose bed to an underground province.
An emerald moth has flattened itself on the window
like a set of poisoned lungs.

A woman weary of such parlour tricks,
she has brought in his head, once again,
on a silver salver.
She will permit
his fortune-teller's palm on her breast
but this evening she sees his fingers
curved and lined, a scallop shell,
a platform for Beauty.

Circus 1907

Bundles of clothes form damp walls,
fencing off the ground where the tall ones sleep.
They gather the bundles up at dawn,
load them on the steaming oiled train,
their faces blanched spots of frost,
their skirts and overalls brushing past me, rubbing
tears, with their roughness, from my eyes.
I have crouched behind these barrels
for days, fed only on sugar-water rags
which the tall ones push into my fingers,
impatient at my whining.
At the next town, the red box
will be unloaded once more, I will
grip the bars and be buried
by the fresh hay shoved through.
As the tall ones lift me into the air
I see the poke-eyed, mushroom faces
of children, leering or crumpling in fear,
the grey sweat of the ringmaster,
the polished muscles straining over me.
The town dwindles to wooden blocks
as, with delight, I loop my body
in the shape of a star, a sweetheart.

2
Who is Us

"Moon, moon, help me! I'm stuck!" –Will, 2

"I'm going to be an answer-not, far out in space." –Will, 3

"Am I thinking what I'm thinking?" –Will, 3

Cygnet Lake

1.

Wood nymph or wasp waist?
Masque or mosh?
In this urban idyll,
encroached on by memory,
I'm already living an afterlife.

Rusted staples crowded
the battered tree torso
from which we freed a flyer,
all black slash and wink.
Think it's faded somewhere in my basement,
filed under "Lefko." Our impresario.
Every poet needs a band.
He left Spadina's dust
for SoCal's blaze.
Most lampposts now concrete,
most flyers online.

I folded those wings
and bowed out.
Took the fire escape
from the top-floor loft
Black velvet dresses
with chipped-tooth zippers
crushed in the musk
of the closet. Makeup blotched
as a back-hand-slapped stamp.
No re-admits,
not now.

Only tea-dancing cups, for me,
and mum cocktails with the hollow-eyed (hush).
Afternoons spent at the Butterfly Ball.
My finery the wrinkled silk lines
at my eyes.

2.

I am all thumbs
with your Thumbelina buttons.
They snag a golden thread.
The hairbrush hurts,
makes smart remarks.

The search for a red crayon.
The search for a red lipstick.

Blankets pool on the dance floor
as we slide. You wriggle
on legs longer than yesterday.
My veins are bee-stung
from your birth.

The sound of your bathwater:
"light pink, like the inside of a shell."
My ears haven't stopped ringing
since I walked home in the dark
tokenless, too too many nights.
Sullied, sulking in the dew.
So I must put you
on repeat.

You drape my necklaces
in the shape of a monstrous bird
with a heart-shaped earring-eye,
random heart-shaped teeth.
That's my girl.

You wake and wince,
"The sun is too flashy.
Turn on the dark again."

When did I lose all these feathers?

Table Fable

A Milky Way of rings.
You tread the boards with your fists
and a pistol-handled knife.

A boat of Venetian glass
sails above, scattering loot
bags of jellyfish candy.
Erased: any traces.
We are all dribblers,
on drab days and good.

This new life
refuses to settle.
All the better, to eat.

Your red hoodie,
a wolf's tongue,
laps the chair slats.

Tapping tabla rhythms,
my mug behind a mug,
I spy the spoof, my spoonfeds.

Small Hours

I am Orpheus to my own Eurydice.
Look back and disappear.

Or, at 4 am, think of nothing
but *Hour of the Wolf*,

of Max von Sydow's sorrow-face,
the drowned boy's shoulder.

Nightingale, rooster, lark, owl.
Night hawks, morning folk.

The security guard nursing
the bouncer and the pilot.

Red-eyes weeping
for the hair of the dog.

My Baby Was Sick All Night
blues. A Delta classic.

I'll sing my scratches
on a—what's it?—telephone.

This heavy black hand-cranked
wallflower that toes the party line.

I do your birthmark inventory
just in case, just in the nick.

All sleep is just a catnap.

I will never graduate from
The School of Late Clocks.

Lullaby of Off-Off-Broadway

The smell of the fingerpaint,
the roar of the trees.
For one week, at two, you called your shoulder,
"My shadow."

Your dad's a song-and-dance man.
Triple threat, elastic face—
sometimes we read it wrong.
No, often.

Simon says, Be a tree!
We are felled by his jokes.
You said, "I hope his good mood
is coniferous,
not deciduous."

Winter Garden: Performances Daily

Red-headed aerialist
wings it
from the pine.
Moon-booted kids
re-enact the lunar landing.
Icicles
look daggers.

I applaud from the stage door.

Year of the Rabbit

For Julia

The cat and the fiddle
said Ha ha ha
Ha ha ha
Ha ha ha
The cat and the cow
said Ha ha ha
And the bunny jumped over the moon.

White rabbit white rabbit
pinch punch-drunk.
A garden of snow lumps
sleeping it off.
The frozen promise
opens one eye.
Slow flakes, snowhere,
breeding suspicion.

Hind legs kick past
a white-flashed hind
up a tree-peopled hill
by the King's Highway.
Continental tail lights wink.

O lucky rabbit's foot,
thumping to tease
the dragon's-belly dancers
sidling iced Spadina.
A shower of gold coins,
loons in scarlet sleeves.
Dim sum snow forts
smoked and sweet within.

At bedtime, I offered her the rabbit
or the lamb.
All ears and eyes
and twitching nose,
she chose the wolf.

Reporting from Night

An off-kilter brick oven
with a soft centre. Stiff limbs
in the kiln of a 2 a.m. bed.
I'm in the fever fight
of my life when I get the call.
Who left these babies here?
Get up, get up,
for the zillionth, for the nonce,
tilt, whisper, "Shhhh
hhhhh." A hiss to soothe.
In truth, a command
or a plea.

Mocking clocks:
the old ones with two tongues,
the one with a blood-red colon.

Everyone in tears.
Everyone asleep.
Then day.

Milk Tooth

"How do the new days and days become the old times?" –Julia, 4

Your head rolls against me
on the pillow, a breathing peach,
stone balloon
warmed by breath,
peony face
on a short weak stalk
I contort myself
so as not to twist.

I look down as you fuse
to my now-vast breast.
You seem distant.
A miniature.

Now 3, you say,
"I'm going into the forest"
then saunter in sock feet
down the telescoping hall,
first handing me binoculars the wrong way round
so that you'll seem far away.

I close one eye, then another.
In the binocular vision of memory
you, always small and tall, at once,
here and there.

In the wide-awake night,
let's visit each floor.
The mad paths we tread,
you a bundle, me stooped.
Old woman carrying a firelog.

At two, gesturing up the stairs,
you say, "Let's go up in the tree."

My sob when you laugh for the first time.
Both our faces masks, surprised to extremes.

A tooth! Beyond time
to be weaned.

Now, at 5, that fairy
takes it back. Leaves a cold coin
to bite.

I had a need to carry.
For company.
For toes to nibble.

Once alone, then never

Imprinted

A snow angel sea lion
makes a cameo appearance,
leaving wrinkles and wings.
Pelt shed,
she is a sylph in striped tights.

Mitten foliage is scattered by the door.
The floor wears many hats.
Jackets flesh out
the rad's glowing bones.

So many feet and hands
catching up to mine.

On the sled hill, you say, "We are running
from our footprints."

Late

Roman numerals circled
a *Rosa Centifolia*
on the archaic-romantic
faux-artifact clock.
You lifted a shaky hand.
So lovely!
To my rosy-fingered baby
we were chime-voiced blurs.

I checked those hands, that face,
all sentiment and soft *tsk*,
between woozy-a.m. feedings,
changings, hallucinations,
"Visiting hours"
and palliative's no-time.

Blossom and quick fade
of a hurtful spring.
We knew beauty's cruelty:
we brought it into the world.
Now we'll see it out.

The stroller was awkward in the narrow room.
Newborn and leave-taker
left me awake
watching hands unclench, toes curl,
hearing baby's breath. And yours.

What did your enormous eyes see behind their lids?
As your breath grew erratic, I tried to slow mine,
counting what you shared:
an extra-long toe on the left foot,
a quick wide smile,

me. As awkward as a teen,
I tried to curve round you,
my limbs like those sentinel numbers.
You the fair rose at the white sheet's centre,
my face, and the sleeping baby, in shadow.

That damn pretty clock.
Each time I check it,
I hear your approval
—delivered in seconds—
over and over
and I hoard it. As if I could.
Our *très riches heures*
ticking away.
It hangs above us still.

Copper Cliff

Pills crushed in sugar,
that hospital's sharp stucco.
Rock candy against the dark
sky, sulphur-stained rock.

My father's cot rattled
like the raw-ore carts.
The chimneys aligned
with the smelter's stacks.

I turned over and over
the penny in my pocket.
Tarnished treasure
in my hot little hand.
What are the prospects?
The paths led nowhere.

No, led to a lilac
that nodded over me.
A well-meaning wordless
aunt in heavy scent.

At the cliff of Copper Cliff,
I thought, over and over.

Lost Taut Line

Cast eye and lip into sleep.
They are lost
but return in the mirror as you lean before it,
as you search the hollows of your body for the line,
the taut line cast down into sleep.

Returning along the lost taut line,
the bodies of sleep propped up around me,
I search in window glass for the lean
familiar hollows, the eye of birch.

The taut grip of your hand is lost
to sleep, so the hollow of my hand searches over
the glass cast, waiting for you to return
and lean over, losing night softness.

Nov. 5:15 pm

For William

"Dance with me!"
Two-year-old tyrant
to his wild-eyed cook
Sun sinks off the menu,
a pool of hot sauce
on a dried-twig bed.
Throbbing head,
water near boiling,
battling arms,
nose at my knee.
OK. We'll dance.
I sweep him up,
my tiny partner
so light off his feet.

Sky dark,
plates bare.
I ask,
"Why did we dance?
"Because because

of the sun
in the music
on the radio."

Snail's Pace

For Nicholas

Hard-candy whorls,
soft sticky skins.
Shell-loving homebodies
shuddered at, devoured.
Wine-soaked and hot,
tickling foot in the mouth,
back in my salad days
—kid-less and ravenous.
S-swallowing my nerves
with a surge of desire.
Food vs. Fear.

My cliché squeals,
my earthy hungers
quieted, I watch you, after rain,
lift them from stems,
from the shy sides of leaves
or from parched pavement.
You palm them, marvel,
then set them rippling,
athrill in a vegetable world.
Eight and in love.
"We put the 'sigh'
in science," you say.

Once-tiny you, a nautilus
I launched, unfurled
to a giant naturalist.
For now, I'll eat them up
only through your eyes.

Morning Kindergarten.

A sunbeam, school-sprung,
rekindles day.
She's a poster painting
of herself.
A splash of sky
blurs her top.
"It's permanent," she sings.
I wish.

Night Cartographer's Song

In time, they all learn
not to roll off
the edge.

It's as if
in sleep
the room is ringed
with monsters
and the world
really is both
flat

and sharp.

Demi-monde

Marker rubbed off
when the kids wobble-traced
their hands and feet.

Now, they wear drawings
of their hands and feet
on their hands and feet.

March Hatter

I am afflicted by tulipomania,
ailurophilia
and an attention headache.

I am at least as confused
as the raccoon drinking
ice water on our deck
in the mid-day sun.

Numb

We raced twig boats in the swelled creek.
Slapstick slip-in-the-mud,
pout, crouch,
the first raw buds above us.
Soakers, sore fingers.
We spent hours
and hours.

Seawater, mud, melt.
No tea, no heat.
All fuel spent.
The school is a makeshift morgue.
The bowling alley is a makeshift morgue.
There's a car on the roof.
Along with ruined tatami
we found vinyl records:
an older person lived here
once.

Between escape and wave,
13 seconds.

Drawing In

Light-enhanced evening
but the breeze has an undertow.

You, 3, point at glossy wood:
"Look! The trees, the pool, the deck, me.
 It's a mystery."

We are sandal-slap happy,
lolling in summer's lap.
Pashas who plash.

Soon, the sky will turn the other blue.

Night Undone

Rain transmissions to our hilltop
through the window screen:
softened earth,
unwrapped leaves,
buds open-mouthed.

Rosy stolen stars
in a jar.

Windows fogged, tear-streaked.

I'm a lilac voluptuary,
a lilac libertine,
drenched, content,
alone.

Martial

Stag beetle stopped
traffic on the sidewalk.
We were buzzed
by a black-winged
dragonfly. Doubled back
for a cicada casing:
mini medieval armour.
Brought it home
in the palm of my hand.

Hawk on the bald treetop:
eagle metonymy

Lake Road Knowledge

Under the humid forehead of the sky
we breathed in fine grains of bracken.
Along parallel dust tracks
cars ambled like bears in the half-light.
You pulled me suddenly off the road
until we were knee-deep in grass,
feeding the passion of mosquitoes.

Stars cast a dense net,
a shoal of fireflies,
over my unschooled gaze.
Feathers from a hawk's kill littered the path,
yellow leaflets air-dropped in a siege.

It was early summer. We had just met.
Someone's laugh crossed the lake,
startling, as close as a kiss on the ear
or red wine spilled on a bare shoulder.
In cottages along the lake's edge
screened porches were lit, like army tents,
for the manoeuvres of summer.

The Near Suburbs

The curtains you inherited, stiff
and aggressively flowered, as in a motel,
frame your departure. Alone, I complete
a grade-school assignment:
how much of the world can be seen
through this strip of glass? Crossing guard,
soundless mouths, delivery van,
weakling trees, skid marks.

An Arthur Murray anthropologist
I track our waltz upstairs and down,
pausing at memorable cushions, counters,
door frames. Even when I stalk your back
my kiss rests neatly between your shoulders.
We fit, at times despite ourselves,
and to the dismay of our smile-free neighbour.
Pearls of wisdom rest just too far
from her ears. With her weed-haired grandkids
she is as nurturing and ruthless as a gardener

Her rival faction to the south,
the Baptist puppeteers,
hold out hope from their van
but our downtown pungency,
our premature wariness,
discourage doorstep conversions.
In the local park, they blushed
at the touching Canadian moment
when I licked the ice from your eyelashes
before you skated to a face-off.
They trust that our childlessness
won't last. They don't suspect
that the snow swirling up in our driveway
with the breadth and uncertainty of a man
causes us to shiver, separately,
or that the smug laundry steam
vented from every other house
may lure us to the humidity
of opposite coasts.

When you return, I rub feeling
into my cheek by nuzzling the cloth
(like spun tobacco) of your dad's old coat.
This houseboat, a frivolous
"San Francisco bungalow"
lacks insulation. The street is ice-choked.
Houses clank and groan at anchor.

Wiskatjan

Curled in the glacial cradle of the rock
we lie like one translucent reed
while whiskey jacks, predictably, mock.
Flecks of mica wink. Back at camp, they read
the story printed on our arms and thighs
in the furtive ink of blueberry stains.
Your irises, swirled, like wings of damselflies.
The scratches on my breasts' soft moraines.
We claim brief treasures from decay, we reach
for warm brown nubs of beer bottle glass
like hoarded sugar sucked smooth by the beach.
The others lose our trail in deep grass.
By the blind white leaves of a poplar tree
the salamander performs its anatomy.

English Drama to 1642

My second-hand bed, on castors,
rolled down the raked floor, amid cat-calls,
to centre stage. Our play began

with the student who fled in tears
from a hothouse seminar
on *The Duchess of Malfi*.
"Heartless, you." Our eyebeams met.
We dropped our fears
among the corridor's squeaks and sighs.

Your second sentence lasted three red lights.
Your gaze grazed my shoe buckle
then wove slowly up my tights
(my dearest, close-knit friends).

You railed at those things that you wanted
from deep in the armchair, deep in the bourbon.
Plague rosettes bloomed on the damask.
Foul papers fell from the printer.
You plotted revenge,
I cradled phantasms.

What seeped and stained beneath the door
might have been the rain, my roommate's tea
or blood from the pages on the floor.

Cooler Heads

Soft spikes and damp ringlets
sluiced and spritzed, flicked and dabbed.

Your silent crashing backstroke
in the pool of our bed.

We scold and protest all afternoon,
grooming the kids with our voices.

Your fingers dawdle through my hair.
Water jewels, rippled sky.

July eyelids eliding
in heat and light.

Barely-toe-dipping.
A thin-skinned kiss.

Thunder amped by the lake.
Petals crumpled. Kids abuzz.

In our deliquescence,
doting. Delinquent
aquamarine.

In Arcadia

The Victorian houses in Toronto's Annex
were long ago redeemed. Bought for a folk song
they now rent out at cruel rates.
The dandelions on the lawn
are not long for this uprooting world.
Like a field of philosophers
their bright ideas have gone up in smoke,
the only consolation of their art
the thought of their thoughts seeding abroad,
up, up and away…

Where are the radical summers?
The fashions are back.
Platform shoes raise the idealistic
a few inches above the pavement.
Shoulders and hair slump
in eco gloom.
I recall the thunder of Riders on the Storm
in the submarine-schoolbus of hippie camp.
Felt pens for never-finished mandala posters,
paper sunbursts, fingers implicated
by indigo tie-dye.
The agit-prop of story-book theatre.
Et in Arcadio ego.
Ergo…

Circling the campfire, we held hands,
sending a ring pulse, swaying in a trance
to melt down selfish private thoughts.
Singing against fears of bears, mosquitoes, lightning,
the military-industrial complex.
A muddle of flower children
in a split-stem chain.

One harsh day, we spray-painted stones
in orange and silver, like makeup in *Seventeen*.
We daydreamed about hurling them
through the black-out curtains of our old-school
school, beneath the heavily framed queen

who reigned over our class.
The focal point of the photograph
was her narrow waist. The garden of her dress
stood corrected by her wasp-nest hair.
She offered pale, empty hands.

Bedtime Story

For Helen Oyeyemi

Scorpions are the smallest dragons,
breathing fire through their tails.

Envoi

I am that swallow swooning around trees in the grey blue, avaricious for twilight, opinionated, uninterested in your lit red-yellow windows and your dinner cooking, in the motorcycle's hyperbole or the squawk of a neighbour's kid out too late, just in the light rain and the pines and the last chance to whirl before you, before dark.

Acknowledgements

Some of these poems first appeared (in slightly different form, in some cases) in the following publications: *London Magazine* (England, ed. Alan Ross), *The Antigonish Review, U.C. Review, Saturday Night, Descant, Grain, Poetry Canada Review, Writing Women* (Newcastle-upon-Tyne, England), *The Toronto Quarterly, The Toronto Star, Poetry'z Own*. Many thanks to the editors.

This book had a long gestation, to say the least. Many people have offered me their encouragement, support and editorial wisdom over the years. My thanks are due to Michael Ondaatje, Mark Strand, Andrew Motion, Fred D'Aguiar, Christopher Dewdney, Karen Mulhallen, Ted Chamberlin, Mark Kingwell, John Ball, the late Michael Dixon, Florence Richler, the late Mordecai Richler, Michael Hofmann, Gary Barwin, Stuart Ross, Mark Truscott, Greg Ioannou, Jeannette Lambert, Gregory Sinclair, Megan Williams, Catherine Graham, Michael Redhill, Nyla Matuk, Carmel Purkis and Helen Oyeyemi.

Thanks to Gregory Betts for his Three Words Per Poem project. I enjoyed participating in it.

Love and thanks to my supportive family members, including Gregory, Jennifer, Stephen, James, Kelci, Jim, Cathy, both Philips and Mary-Eileen.

The financial support of the Ontario Arts Council, through a Works-in-Progress grant and a Writer's Reserve grant, is deeply appreciated.

The epigraph for Part 1 is the first line of "A Certain Tree in Powązki Cemetary" by Piotr Sommer, from *Things to Translate & Other Poems*, Bloodaxe Books, 1991. The poem was translated by Piotr Sommer and John Ashbery.

Many thanks to Douglas Walker for permitting the use of his beautiful painting on the cover.

In "Late," "très riches heures" is a reference to a medieval Book of Hours, Les Très Riches Heures du Duc de Berry: an exquisite illuminated manuscript painted by the Limbourg brothers, Paul, Hermann and Jean for Jean, Duc du Berry.

Iguana Books
iguanabooks.com

If you enjoyed *Reporting from Night* ...
You can learn more about Kateri Lanthier and her upcoming work on her blog.
katerilanthier.iguanabooks.com/blog/

If you're a writer ...
Iguana Books is always looking for great new writers, in every genre. We produce primarily ebooks but, as you can see, we do the occasional print book as well. Visit us at iguanabooks.com to see what Iguana Books has to offer both emerging and established authors.
iguanabooks.com/publishing-with-iguana/

If you're looking for another good book ...
All Iguana Books books are available on our website. We pride ourselves on making sure that every Iguana book is a great read.
iguanabooks.com/bookstore/

Visit our bookstore today and support your favourite author.
iguanabooks.com

www.ingramcontent.com/pod-product-compliance
Lightning Source LLC
LaVergne TN
LVHW041235080426
835508LV00011B/1223